START-UP
DESIGN AND TECHNOLOGY

VEHICLES

Louise and Richard Spilsbury

Evans

Published by Evans Brothers Limited
2A Portman Mansions
Chiltern Street
London W1U 6NR

© Evans Brothers Limited 2006

Produced for Evans Brothers Limited by
White-Thomson Publishing Ltd.,
Bridgewater Business Centre, 210 High Street,
Lewes, East Sussex BN7 2NH

Printed in China by WKT Company Limited

Editor: Dereen Taylor
Consultants: Nina Siddall, Head of Primary School
Improvement, East Sussex; Norah Granger, former
primary head teacher and senior lecturer in Education,
University of Brighton
Designer: Leishman Design

British Library Cataloguing in Publication Data
Spilsbury, Louise
    Vehicles. - (Start-up design and technology)
    1. Vehicles - Juvenile literature
    I. Title II. Spilsbury, Louise
    629.2

ISBN: 0 237 53026 0
13-digit ISBN (from 1 Jan 2007) 978 0 237 53026 6

Acknowledgements:
Special thanks to the following for their help and
involvement in the preparation of this book: Staff
and pupils at Coldean Primary School, Brighton;
Elm Grove Primary School, Brighton; Hassocks
Infants School, Hassocks.

Picture Acknowledgements:
Chris Fairclough Worldwide 5; TopFoto 6.
All other photographs by Chris Fairclough.

Artwork:
Tom Price, age 8, page 7; Hattie Spilsbury, age 10,
page 19.

Contents

Looking at vehicles

Vehicles transport people or things from one place to another. There are lots of different kinds of vehicles travelling on the road.

▼ What are the names of the vehicles in this picture?

Can you think of any other kinds of vehicles?

vehicles   transport   travelling

◄ **Ambulances are vehicles that take people to hospital.**

Who uses these other vehicles and what do they use them for? Why are these vehicles different shapes?

ambulances   shapes

Old car, new car

Sunil's grandpa has brought his car to school. It is old and special.

HLU 894K

◀ Katy's mum has brought in her new car.

How are these vehicles different?
How are they the same?

6

labels   wheels

▼ Sunil draws a car and labels the different parts.

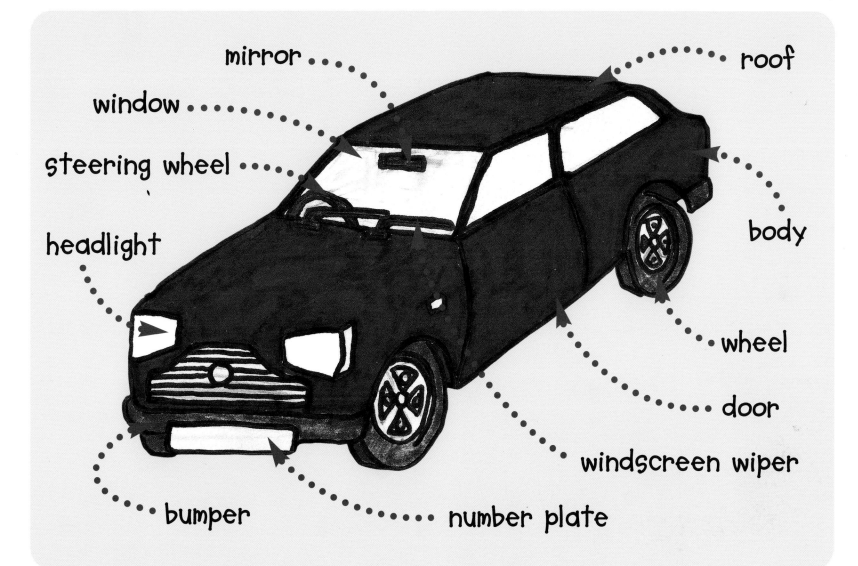

mirror

window

steering wheel

headlight

roof

body

wheel

door

windscreen wiper

bumper

number plate

Why do cars have wheels?

Why do cars have headlights and bumpers?

What kind of car would you draw?

headlights   **bumpers**

Wheels go round

Heidi's class has been singing 'The wheels on the bus go round and round'.

▶ Heidi pushes the toy bus to make its wheels go round. When the wheels go round, the bus moves.

When Heidi pushes harder, the bus goes faster. A push is a kind of force.

pushes   moves   faster   force

An axle connects pairs of wheels to a vehicle. Wheels and axles can be joined in two different ways.

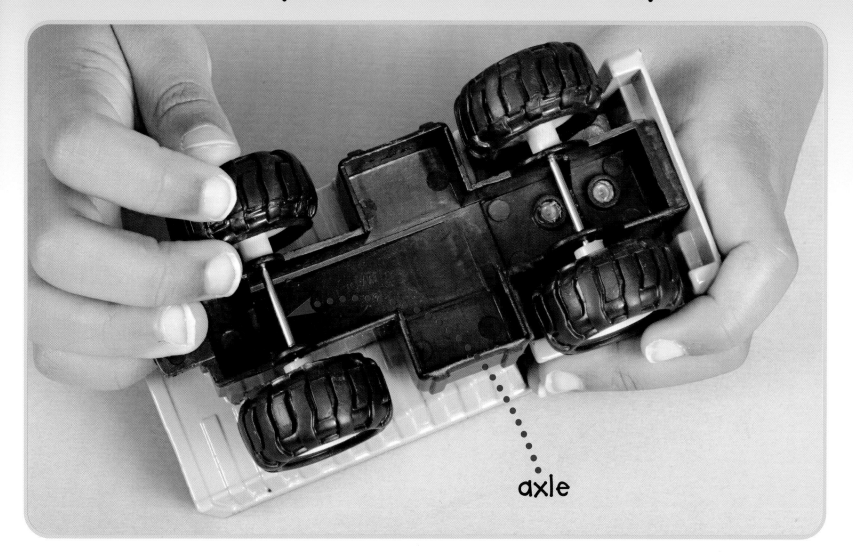

axle

Some vehicles have axles that move the wheels. The wheels are fixed to the axles. Other vehicles have fixed axles. The wheels rotate around the axles.

axle   connects   fixed   rotate   9

Making a pull-along cart

Ben is making a cart to pull his sister's rabbit along.

▲ He uses a plier punch to make four holes in a box and pushes two straws through, to make axles.

▲ He attaches wheels to the axles and holds them in place with Plasticine.

cart   pull   plier punch

◀ **He uses tape to stick some string to the front of the cart.**

Materials and tools
- plier punch • cardboard box
- straws • wheels • Plasticine
- tape • string

▶ **Ben pulls the cart along to check if the wheels turn smoothly.**

Does Ben's cart do the job it was made for?
How could Ben improve his model?

smoothly   improve   model

Moving a floor turtle

When people are driving a car, they turn a steering wheel to make it change direction.

▶ Fi wants a floor turtle to move towards different objects. She writes down instructions to give the turtle.

direction   instructions   forwards

▶ **Fi would like the turtle to move forwards. She presses the forward button 3 times.**

▼ **She selects 'Go' and watches the turtle move towards the drums.**

Can you program a floor turtle to make it move?

selects   program

Making a go-kart

Sol wants to make a go-kart that he can steer.

Materials and tools
- card • cotton reels • tape
- split pin • string • straws
- Plasticine • match box
- plier punch • toy figure

▲ Sol makes holes in two pieces of card using a plier punch. He joins them together using a split pin.

▲ He sticks straw axles to the card with tape.

go-kart   steer

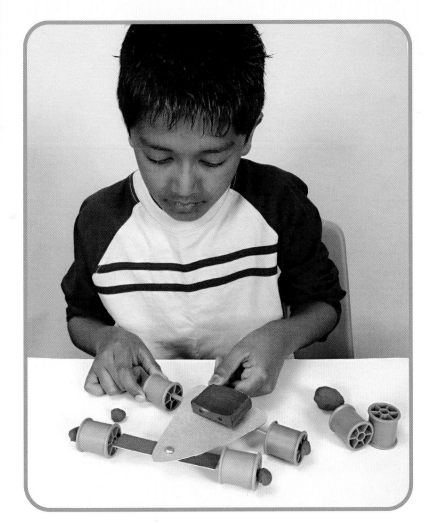

▲ Sol sticks on a matchbox for the seat. He has made two holes in it. He uses cotton reels for wheels. He adds Plasticine to keep them on the axles.

▼ He connects the front bar and the seat with string. What happens when Sol pulls one of the strings?

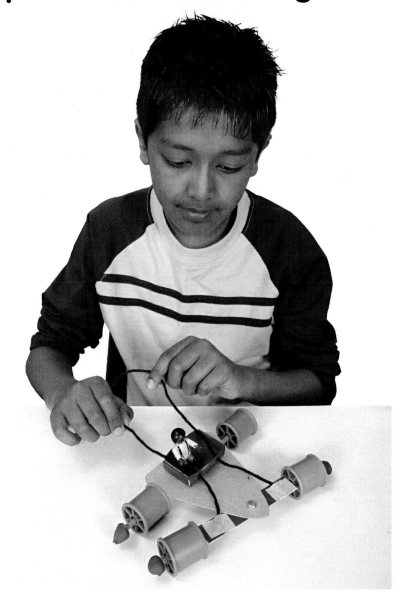

Vehicles on the move

Miles and Hattie are rolling vehicles down a ramp. They start at the top of the ramp each time. They use a metre rule to measure how far the vehicles go.

ramp   metre rule   measure   distance

▼ They add bricks to make the ramp steeper. Then they measure the distance again.

▶ Miles and Hattie make a block graph to show their results.

Have they made sure it is a fair test? What might change how far the vehicles go?

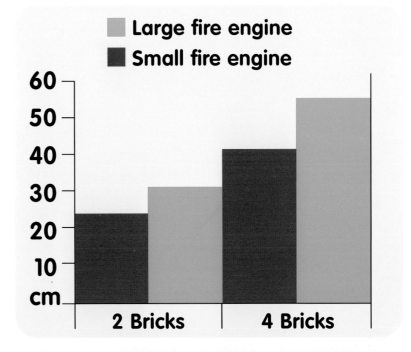

Large fire engine
Small fire engine

	2 Bricks	4 Bricks

60
50
40
30
20
10
cm

block graph   results   fair test   17

Planning a new van

Zena's uncle sells cookies.
She wants to **design** a delivery van for him.

◀ Zena looks at a model vehicle to give her ideas. She plans to have doors at the back of her model for **loading** the cookies. She thinks about how the doors might open.

design   loading   sketch

Zena makes a sketch of her design and plans the materials she will use. Why has she chosen transparent plastic for the window?

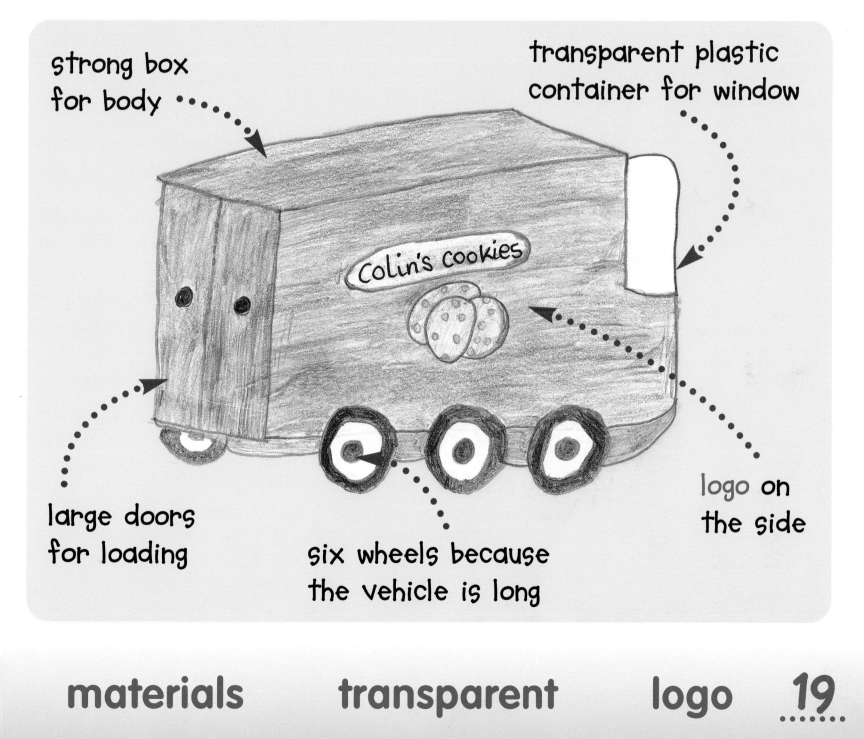

strong box
for body

transparent plastic
container for window

Colin's cookies

large doors
for loading

six wheels because
the vehicle is long

logo on
the side

Making the van

Zena has painted her model van red because that is her uncle's favourite colour.

▲ She cuts the back of the box and folds the two halves of card to make the hinge doors.

▲ She adds glue to the sides of the window and sticks it in to the front of the van.

▼ Zena designs a logo on the computer. She cuts it out and checks if it is the right size for the van.

▼ Zena thinks it improves her model if the logo is bigger. What do you think?

Materials and tools
- box • paints • Plasticine
- straws • plastic container
- glue • wheels • scissors
- computer

Does the model match Zena's design? Why do you think this is?

checks   size

Further information for

New words listed in the text:

ambulances	design	headlights	moves	sketch
axle	direction	hinge	plier punch	smoothly
block graph	distance	improve	program	steer
body	fair test	instructions	pull	transparent
bumpers	faster	labels	pushes	transport
cart	fixed	loading	ramp	travelling
checks	force	logo	results	vehicles
computer	forwards	materials	rotate	wheels
connects	go-kart	measure	selects	
		metre rule	shapes	
		model	size	

Possible Activities

PAGES 4–5
Children could watch the road outside their school and write down the different kinds of vehicles they see. This is also a good opportunity to talk about road safety.

Children could write down the names of as many vehicles designed to carry different loads as they could think of, such as a coach, tractor, refuse truck and wheelbarrow.

Collect pictures of different kinds of vehicles and ask children what type of person they think would drive them.

PAGES 6–7
Read a story about an old-fashioned style car with the children, such as Brum or Gumdrop. Or perhaps an elderly relative could come in to talk to the class about how vehicles have changed.

Children could draw a vehicle on the computer and then label its different parts. They could extend labels with a description of what each part is used for. For example, headlights are used at night so drivers can see where they are going.

PAGES 8–9
Children could examine and group a selection of toy vehicles with the two different kinds of axles and wheels to help them understand the difference.

Give children a selection of pictures of vehicles with different numbers of wheels and discuss why different vehicles have different numbers of wheels.

Encourage children to think about forces and movement, and how things move.

PAGES 10–11
Children could make a model car using construction kits. Encourage children to assess their own models and each other's. Could they improve them by decorating them, making them sturdier, making sure the finish was neater, etc.

How could they decorate a model vehicle made from reclaimed materials to make it look fun to use? Who would they make a model for?

Parents and Teachers

PAGES 12–13

Talk to the children about the many kinds of machines and devices that follow instructions, such as washing machines and photocopiers. They could also look at pictures of devices such as the Mars rover, which follows instructions from Earth to explore Mars.

PAGES 14–15

Make a land yacht with a basic chassis with axles and wheels. Then add a stick to the chassis for a mast and attach a scrap fabric sail. Children could use a hairdryer or fan to blow the land yachts along.

PAGES 16–17

Discuss with the children the factors that make a test fair – are the vehicles the same size, are they starting at the same point each time, are they being pushed with the same force? Make a list of the things that might affect how far/fast vehicles go.

Do a test about friction. Children could push (and let go) a car over two or three different surfaces, such as wood, carpet, corrugated cardboard or rough concrete. Discuss why the car goes furthest over the smoothest surface.

PAGES 18–19

Children could plan to include other kinds of moving parts in their vehicles, such as steering wheels, windows that open and tipping bodies.

Children could make sketches, lists of materials and numbered plans of the order in which they intend to make their model.

PAGES 20–21

Children could try other ways of decorating and finishing vehicles, such as collage. Encourage children to assess their own and each other's work. Does it look like the plan? Discuss how sometimes it is hard to actually implement creative ideas and, picking one example, ask the children to come up with solutions and alternatives.

Further Information

BOOKS FOR CHILDREN

Cars (Oxford Reds) by Paul May (Oxford University Press, 2000)

Fire Engines (Big Machines) by Penny and David Glover (Franklin Watts, 2004)

Forces and Movement (Start-up Science), Claire Llewellyn (Evans, 2004)

Little Nippers: Let's Go By Bus, by Barbara Hunter (Heinemann Library, 2002)

Toy Cars by Wendy Sadler (Heinemann, 2005)

Trucks (Young Machines) by H. Castor (Usborne Publishing Ltd. 2004)

WEBSITES

www.eriding.net/dandt/index.shtml

www.primaryresources.co.uk/art

www.sciencemuseum.org.uk/education

Index